woke

adjective
(past of wake)

1. emerged or caused to emerge from a state of sleep; stopped sleeping.
"She woke up."

•became alert to or aware of.
"She woke up to reality."

•caused (something) to stir or come to life.
"She woke desire in others."

2. alert to and concerned about social injustice and discrimination.

"She's an activist and very woke."

Woke

What does it mean to be "woke"?

SHAYLA BROWN

Shayla Brown is a writer, editor, and publisher on the rise. She is also the author of poetry books, Thoughtspoken: Writing Out Loud, Little Brunch Queen: Poetry for the babies of the mamas from the 90s & 80s, and Brunch Queen: Brunch poetry…for the culture.

Visit Shayla-Brown.com to follow her creative writing and to read more of her published work.

Shayla Brown is also the creator and senior editor of The Genesis Birthing and Living "Black Birth Story Blog: Where Black Women are the authority on Black Birth", and the creator and executive producer of the Genesis Birthing and Living "Listening to Black Women" YouTube series.

This is for you.

Table of Contents

12 YEARS BLEEDING

"Take heart, daughter," he said, "your faith has healed you."

Matthew 9:22

Sleep

If you're looking for us
We'll be in the trees

Hiding
            Blamed
Shamefully

Hiding our heads
Dressed in black
Hiding our flair
Cov'rin our backs
Manipulating
Cov'rin our tracks.
Gossiping
Handing out flack.

Prayer warrior busy bodies
Practicing witchcraft.

Faithfully following
imposter prophets
down
a dangerous path.

"And so, because baby's skin was two or three shades darker than Rebecca's, it gave her the right of choosing her for her own, as you would a kitten."

—The Little Slave Girl

Like kittens they were–
the babes of her slaves–
of every weight,
and of every shade.

But few–if any–
were half as pretty
as Hattie's girl ninny;
nor were as giddy.

So without a smile,
the young mistress prowled,
and stood over Hattie
demanding her child.

"You won't her, Missy?"
Hattie asked briskly.
"Yes," said lil' Missy.
"She's cute and she's pretty."

And with that she left
to get her Father's help
to finalize her theft
and enjoy her wealth.

But Hattie sewed on.

Her spirit was long gone.

Her family was long torn.

She couldn't even feel scorn.

Cause since she was born:

- Her mother was sold
- Her father was cold
- She never had a family household.

She did not hope for

a daughter with more
because
she was
historically
poor.

Her poor little baby
A poor victim of slavery.
Trodden down daily,
Hattie went crazy.

She would be beauty
anywhere else.

But here she is only

an en route to wealth.

Selma, Lord, Selma

A little girl

held by her hand
walked into a dangerous band;
a national fight;
a toiling land.

A little girl

encouraged to stand.

Little girls;
marching like men;
bombed and tear-gassed;
hunted black skin.

She just had a realization:

All her days she'd been maid
to care for others without being paid.

Care added cooking but added no raise.

All her life then she'd been a slave.

Sustenance

Benefits

But no handheld wage.

No money in her hands

She never was paid

Only was she ever stored and locked away
With no keys to life
Alone and afraid.

Talks With Elder Women Be Like:

You little stupid whore.

These boys don't care bout you.

They want to see how their thing works
They want to practice too.

These little boys only want
the thing there in your pants.
You think he will stay satisfied
with only holding hands?

And that's why you're forbidden, girl
and not allowed to go
not allowed to bud or blossom
not allowed to grow.

You're allowed only
to stay here and stay slow.

Cover up your body, girl!
You're not allowed to show.

Look how wide your hips have got
You clearly are a hoe
A slut
A bitch
A thot
A trick
A fast tail 304.

Why Don't Black Women Ever Ask For Help?

It's not that we don't ask,
It's that we aren't obliged.

It's not that we don't ask
It's that we are *denied*.

It's not that we don't ask—
Believe me—we've *tried*,
Believe me, we've *begged*
Believe me, we've cried.

"Believe me," we ask.

Believe me—
We try
Believe me–we beg
believe me, we cry.

"BELIEVE ME!" we cry
and then with a sigh,
we lose belief,
and then you ask "why".

Why Don't Black Women Ever Accept Help?

Because
We are offered in jest.

As if to suggest
That our need is from something *lacking* in us.
Something that makes us
Somehow
Less than
enough.

Not because
the task at hand
is too much for any woman

(*Or* any man).

But because
Somehow
Though time and again
From sunrise to sunset
Day out and day in
We grow thicker skin…

We are offered only in jest
As if to suggest
That our need is from something *lacking* in us
That makes us,
Instead,
Less than enough.

So fuck…

"I'll do it myself."

Mean Girls

Until you've held blood-stained pants…
(No
You can't sit with us)

Held them things stretched cross your hands…
(No
You can't sit with us)

Until you've been betrayed by your very best friends
Over male attention
Gotten in fights and got detention
Had to fight older men not to mention
Been blamed as the victim…

You can't sit with me.

Until you've had a sore, budding chest
And jest aimed at you for new budding breast
And pinched popped back
From bra string attack
From boys in your class who sit at your back
Been group-groped and attacked
Scared to fight back—NO
YOU CAN'T SIT WITH ME!

You've already taken everything else!
Now you want to take that??
Can women please have womanhood back?
No?
We *can't?*

Shattered Illusions

Country and poor.

I thought I were more.

than dirty feet
across dirt floor

than dust tracks on dirt roads
Than baskets-filled
laundromat loads
And mold humble abodes…

Than UnGodly
And Unclean
(Although always cleaning everything)

Than Delta swamps
and Wetlands

Than "Mississippi Goddamn"
Than: got levees but ain't got no dams

Than sharing spouses
And swapping' husbands
Than backwoods babies
And kissin' cousins

I got college educated
So I thought I got elevated
I prematurely celebrated
Cause I thought I was more

Than Mississippi country
Dirt roads
And dirt poor

Than just a little country girl
with just a country sound
from nowhere in the whole wide world
From just a country town.

Inequality

As a man
I expect
That I will know
And you will agree.

(As a woman
 I expect
that I will wait
And you will see…)

Woke

I never felt so small…

[as when
I found out
I was black.]

Never felt as worthless as when:

I knew
of all its lack.

Never felt this hopeless
unTill:

seeing my sons' faces…

After:

discrimination

by defected
racists.

You can call me crazy
  (If that's what you'd like to do.)

    You can call me delusional,
       (And other names too.)

You can try
and deny
that any of this
includes you,
but what you can't deny
is that:
            what I say
            is true.

We Bare the Mask

The hand that holds the glass ceiling
mocks our peeks up at its building.
The bet is that we will defile
our selves and mourn our domicile,
and just mouth myriad subtleties.

Why shouldn't the world be over-wise,
In counting all our tears and sighs?
Yay, let them only see us, while
        We bare the mask.

With guile, it disregards our cries
With glee, it hands out canned replies.
It stings, but oh! Karma is wild!
You reap just what you sew in style.
Keep on dreaming otherwise, but
        We bare the mask!

Sympathy

I'm angry I'm pregnant
      (And afraid to be)

I'm Angry

That when I speak
      I'm diversity

Angry
At marginalized creativity

I'm angry at shootings in my community

Angry
at Medicaid-grade therapy.

I'm angry at my fucked up family's piss-poor poverty

I'm angry.

I worry constantly.

Does no one know what it's like to be me:

      tired of being Black
wanting to be free?

LOCKS

                  My hair is stronger together.
Together it's better grown.

the strands are more vulnerable dangling alone.

the strands will struggle hanging on their own:

        Tossed about with every wind and frivolously blown.
A flying seed unsown;
a broken-winged bird unflown;

           my hair is too unstrong
           to take constant comb.

It can't take disruption;
or parting and interruption.

Strands can't stand abandoned
stranded under heavy-handed—

                        together
                      they throng.

                     Flocked like birds
                       flying

                  and getting along.

A Black Girl Speaks of Writing

Where can I be black?

And a poet

at that?

Reparations?

I

My grandfather was a member of the Klu Klux Klan.
He was personally responsible for killing a young woman
and
a young man.

How can I repay lives lost?
How can I repay?

A priceless cost.

II

My mother died.
Left boxes piled high.
Deep in her basement
relics survived.

I found a ledger
A list of names
Detailed descriptions
detailing slaves.

III

Land
claimed.
Stolen though,
from our slaves.

So I unfollowed my family's tracks…

found the actual owners…

then gave it back.

SUFFER LITTLE CHILDREN

"Suffer little children, and forbid them not, to come unto me: for of such is the Kingdom of Heaven."

Matthew 19:14; Luke 18:16

Unconscious Bias

In new teacher training,
we learned to first build
positive relationships
before forming skills.

We should:

- **Communicate** positive expectations.
- **Reduce** stress and frustrations.
- **Correct** our students in a *constructive* way.
- Use these strategies every day.

We should:

- be empathetic
- positive and energetic
- smile and build trust
- let our students see *us*

- Kill dead time
- to minimize disruption
- create student-centered/
- oriented instruction
- Restore
- broken teacher-
- student relationships
- following our 6
- communication steps

"Now class," says the trainer,
"Our student was rude.
He's finished his work
He's in a bored mood.

He finished his test
drummed on his desk
it bothered his teacher
she called him a pest.

Jumping up, hurt,
he started to fume.
He pushed past his teacher
to leave the room.
She blocked the door,

he couldn't move.
She called an officer
he was removed.

This student is black.

What different things
could the the teacher do?"

Looking around
most confused,
the room paused…

"We have no clue."

Fire

All her life she's had to *fight*
just for the *opportunity* to be right.
just to oblige *her own* insight.
She's had to wrestle with angels for light.

Just because she likes
to read and to write
She gets told
that she acts white.

She's a smart girl
trapped beneath blight
imprisoned in poverty
dreaming of flight.

A caged bird beating with all of her might
the cruel bars restricting her
and gripping her tight.

Puppies From Pounds

Children in cages

varying in ages.

Roundup rampages
Of workers of low wages

      (been here for ages)

snatched.
separated:

      Children from parents like books ripped of pages.

Oh?

You thought my silence was compliance?

Little did *you* know.

It was defiance.

Only a child,
I was only surviving.

I'm no longer yours
and now I'm thriving.

I'm no longer yours
no longer dying.

(Maybe some tears
Might be some crying.)

No longer yours,
I'm no longer lying.

Only the truth
I'm no longer hiding.

no longer flailing
finally prevailing

No longer falling
finally
I'm flying.

Silenced

In my dream I was writing.
Papers strewn everywhere.
I sat—young and adolescent—
at the table
in the kitchen
of the trailer
of my childhood home;
smiling, but alone.

In my dream I wore a dress;
a flower down the middle.
It fit—long and comfortable—
on the body
along the curves
of the frame
of my preteen build;
modest, but revealed.

My hair was neatly pulled back;
a ponytail down my neck.
I stood, shocked and flabbergasted
at the scratch
on the back door
of the trailer
of my childhood home;
frightened, and alone.

A determined yellow cat
clawing at the black screen door;
it clung, crossed and unrelenting
to the truth
in the writing
on the papers
chronicling my life—
peculiar, but rife.

Before,
on the porch—
not the front, but the back–
there a farmer
with a dark gray hat
by his black truck
subtly sat
feeding a large snake

long, big, and black.

His only intent,
to divert and distract.
A few times over,
I fell for his trap...

But then...

I went in.

Through the back door
to begin
writing.

Papers strewn.
Young and adolescent.
At the table.
In the kitchen
of the trailer
of my childhood home;
smiling, but alone.

Regret

The more She thinks on what She did
The more cause for regret.
Pressured by him,
She moved too soon.

She wasn't ready yet.

Preachers
And teachers;
Seminars to warn;
Disease displayed as threat:

"Legs closed," fingers wagged;
flee premarital sex.

But Why?

She never asked.

Why?

They never told.

Only did they fuss.
Only did they scold.

Her father even asked
"How will you know?"
When boys move too fast,
Will you move too slow?"

The very thought now,
Disgust and a sigh
Boys never lovers
Between each young thigh.

A girl violated
Cringes and cries
Sore, torn vagina
Love that's a lie.

Players;
a game;
All for a name

Hi-fives and handshakes
His victory,
Her shame

And they are all kids though.
So…

Who,
really,
is to blame?

Erasure

In that place, where they tore the nightshade and blackberry patches from their roots to make room for the Medallion City Golf Course, there was once a neighborhood. It stood in the hills above the valley town of Medallion and spread all the way to the river. It is called the suburbs now, but when black people lived there it was called the Bottom.

— Toni Morrison, Sula, 1973[1]

Marieval Indian Residential Boarding School

"The white child may be educated in the affairs of life and life's duties to a great extent without ever entering the doors of a school. The example and precepts of its elders, the contact of its fellows, all the circumstances of its existence are educational agencies, indeed, it is from these far more than from instruction in schools that it learns its duties to God, to the State and to itself. All such circumstances of life equally educate the Indian child at home but its parents, fellows and existence being Indian, it is trained in Indian life not in the life of the white man upon a knowledge of which its future existence depends".-- Lawrence Vankoughnet, Deputy Superintendent General of Indian Affairs in Ottawa

"They made us believe we didn't have souls."
150,000
children
stole.

Ruled a cultural genocide
Catholic Church, apologize.

135 years of theft
(Few Native American communities left).

Insufferable

physical and sexual abuse

Curriculum designed to shrink and reduce

Strict rules imposed
restricting the use
of Indigenous languages
children strangled in
collars attachable and tight like a noose.

Elegy For Native Children Found In Mass in Unmarked Graves At
Catholic Residential Schools

"Genocide cannot be undone or healed overnight."

--Lincoln McKeon; Bishop, Territory of the People

I want you to know
my heart
is breaking for you

and for the
brokenness
of legacy too.

Native children missing;
No good explanation;
Native families abruptly abridged;
creation abbreviation.

Perpetual pogrom.
Assimilationist schools.
Chaotic Catholics;
unconstrained by rules.

Forty one THOUSAND

Dead.

MASSive quarts of tiny blood
shed.

fatal mistreatment
vile neglect
rampant disease—
Accidents?

An "oops" apology?
To settle the debts?

An uneven balance!
Utterly blasphemous!

The Scream, 2017.

Painting On Acrylic Canvas By Kent Monkman

"Indian children should be withdrawn as much as possible from the parental influence, and the only way to do that would be to put them in central training industrial schools where they will acquire the habits and modes of thought of white men."—Sir John A. MacDonald

Against a blue but darkening sky
three birds watch free:

the catholic church in long black cloths

and,

state issued-military,

kidnapping children
from native land
where these birds fly
where these folks stand.

Cries.
No mercy.
Crosses on their necks.
Red,
uniformed bodies.
No natural respect.

Babies flailing
half-dressed and wailing
teens; runaways
escaped; but strays.

Guns in position; ready to shoot
any protest of pillage and loot.

Families robbed like trees robbed of fruit.
Children transplanted like trees from the root.

Erasure

Erasure looks different in the digital age.

It's absence;
omission;
a missing web page.

It's inserting your search—
your Mississippi Home—
and after much searching,
finding you're gone.

It's places you frequent
that *you* know exist,
but somehow,
for some reason,
don't make the list.

It's

click

after

click—
blatant dismiss?

as *if?*

your hometowns

just don't

exist?

It's anger and rage
you *try* to sit with,
it's *your* fam,
And *your* friends —
personal offense.

It's Young
white
hipsters—
new to this place—

with algorithmic autonomy
and power to erase.

It's internet bypasses that
bypass right by you

past strings of towns;
once passed through.

These
southern
little
towns
Little black cocoons
havens in the Jim Crow south
now silently removed.

Where Mamie Till was protected
Where T.R.M Howard was respected
Where the Taborian Hospital
And the nation's first HMO was erected.

Freedmen's towns
Politically free

Functioning
now struggling

Municipalities

Battling
deconstructive
Intentionality
and
allegation
of criminality

It's bigger than Harlem gentrification
It's covered up towns tourist destinations

Dissolving
Displacing
Physically erasing
Developers redeveloping
Governments reshaping

It's an economic issue
where investments lose value.
A way to redistribute
rights, rewards, and revenue.

With acres of Redlining,
And bias in Home Buying...

Revitalization
leaders and organizations
lobbying for state and federal donations
must be in place
to
make the best financial decisions.

Whether it's:

protection from climate change
or preserving their existence.

In some towns,
locals focus
on cultural tourism

(despite lack of provision).

It gives agency over history
and pathway to
bring in revenue
and improve
these conditions.

And that's why erasure now looks different

in the digital age.

It's absence.
omission.
A missing web page.

It's inserting your search—
your Mississippi Home—
and after much searching,
finding it's gone.

It's places you frequented
that you *know* existed,
but somehow,
for some reason,
didn't get listed.

It's

click

after

click—

It's *blatant*
dismiss

as *if*

your hometowns

just don't

exist.

It's anger
and it's rage
you *try*
to sit with.
But it's *your* friends,
And *your* fam —
It's *personal.*
It's offense.

It's Young
white
hipsters—
new to this place—
with algorithmic autonomy
and *power*
to *erase.*

It's internet bypasses
that bypass right by you

past strings of towns;
once passed through.

Psalms, Hymns, and Spiritual Songs

"speaking to yourselves in psalms and hymns and spiritual songs, singing and making melody in your heart to the Lord…"

Ephesians 5:19-24

TESTIMONY

Lil' Debbie snacks used to hit!
'Til I realized them thangs made me *sick*.

Every month—
bleeding and throwing a fit.
Tried ta have a baby but
couldn't get pregnant.

I had acne everywhere!

I even loss some uh my hair;

But I was way too scared
to trust
them doctors for my care.

Asked the healing woman instead;
then I asked the root man.
Cause if anyone can heal me,
them two sho' can.

They said:
"take them packages,
And throw them out thuh doe!
And don't put that mess
inside yo' body no moe!

Eat some harvest food
that grow straight out the ground,

Cause that's where yo nutr'ents
and yo healing is found."

Well I tell yall!

They sho nuff knowed the truth!

I went home and did ev'rythang they tol' me to;
and jus' like they said,
my suffering' was through!
Had me one baby,
Then I had 2!

Praise be ta God!

And Hallelu!
Yawe did it fa me!
He'll do it for you!

A PROPHETIC DREAM

Coffee cups and suits.
Offices white and blue.
Men in black bearing guns;
storm in
and form a coup.

They send you to the back
and serve you spoiled food.
Dirty dishes everywhere–
more work to do.

So now your door is open.
With no defense or might.
Because you have no inclination.
nor intent to fight.

Big bright screen.
Electrifying light.
Neglect and abuse;
become your children's plight.

Wolves–
disguised as helpers–
charge you for prey.
Exposing their fangs,
when you drive away.

PSALM 82:1-6

Today I prayed.

Not to the God of the Universe
to inquire what He could do to bring me peace;
But to the God in me
to inquire what *She*
could do
instead.

PROVERBS 31 WOMAN

"Her children rise up and call her blessed"

I am a comforter,
A nurturer,
A warm smile and a dependable hug.

I am a kind ear and an open heart;
An inventor and keeper of traditions.

I'm a presence,
An advocate,
A teacher—

Submitted,
Powerful,
Bold,
Abundant,
Generous,

I AM

Helpful,
Loving,
Joyful,
Peaceful,
Patient,
Gentle,
Obedient,
Faithful,
Humble,
Disciplined;

and I trust that God the Father,
"from whom are all things",
"Who is over all and through all and in all",
"Father of the fatherless and protector of the widows"

will provide what I can't.

PSALM 46:10

I am strong.
I am magical, too.
I conceived the land,
and the sky,
and the ocean blue.

I am creative.
I Birthed woman,
and man…
and everything that creepeth
across the dirt and the sand.

I am powerful, Baby!
I willed the flood waters down!
I made the disbelieving sorry,
and I bid the wicked drown.

I pulled back the waters,
to let the people pass through;
guided them through the wilderness,
to the promised land too!

But For all my power,
and the respect I'm due,
little more is given,
than half-hearted "thank you".

The compassionate are far between.
The understanding are few.
The Gentiles have more faith in me
than my own children do.

Yes I am strong...
but on the 7th day, didn't I rest?
And don't I spare the beloved
and righteous
the few
who pass my tests?

AND–
despite your iniquities–
don't I give you my best?
Don't I keep my hands stayed on you
so you're favored and blessed?

YES.

Yes!

And faithfulness is my only request,

with fervor and zest,

I ask of thee;

Only;

thy faithfulness.

1 CORINTHIANS 11:15

No.
You can't run your fingers through my hair…

But you *can* grab it and grip it.

You can't easily damage,
tear it,
or rip it.

It's warm and it's thick—
(*soft enough to lay in*).

It's mesmerizing
and tantalizing
tempting you to play in.

It's better when it's clean—
with no smell or sweat.
It's easier to work in
when it's slippery and wet.

I keep it covered sometimes.
sometimes I let it breathe.
I cut it low sometimes;
sometimes I let it be.

My hair…
I like to braid it.
Finger it and penetrate it.
Look at it in the mirror daily
Whip it back and forth and shake it.

Black hair.

My hair.

My crown and my glory.
A preeminent part
of my personal story.

It's a personal gift;

from the Most High above.

And the Most High
gave the most supply
to the most adored
and most loved.

PERSONIFICATION

Everything in the Universe is constantly at Love…

The Sun makes love to the Waters,
Heat rises,
then the Rain and dripping Mountain Tops flow into Oceans and Seas.

Atmospheric Gasses bind to each other in pulsating thrusts,
then gently bloowww
in a soothing breeze.

Something beautiful is born every time Universal Love is made.

Trees erect to pierce The Sky and hit the spot-light
—just right—
covering The Earth in Shade.

Something beautiful is born every time Universal Love is made.

Rock Hard Stones are born from firm, steady Rubbin
Gravitational Pull is born from unrestricted Kissin and Huggin.

Cycles of The Tide shed from The Land to ensure Earth's womb is fertile and black.
Seeds drop from the cocked stems of elevated Plants to ensure Earth's womb is pregnant and fat.

Volcanoes erupt.

Flowers blossom and bloom.

The raised Sun's sun rays probe and saturate Darkness
and are reproduced by The Moon.

Everything is at Love.

Love births Life.
Copulation is the mother of Creation.
Mother Nature is Father Time's wife.

Everything is at Love.
Barren is the end of Life.
Death is the father of Destruction.
Alpha is Omega's wife.

Appreciate Life,
or else
she will fade.

Do not haphazardly blow up in Her;
Do not forcefully invade.

Compassionately enter the circle of Life.

And *feel* how you fit inside her.

Find your position;
hold her tight.
Grip her firmly…
gently ride her.

AFFIRMATION

With bowed head and lowered eyes,
she retreated to the alter of herself.

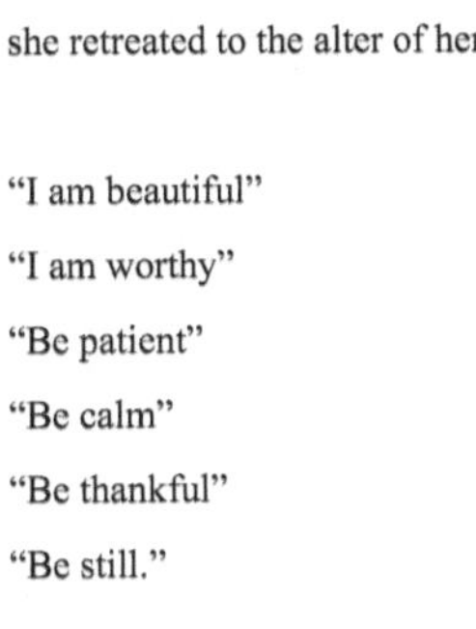

"I am beautiful"
"I am worthy"
"Be patient"
"Be calm"
"Be thankful"
"Be still."

"I am beautiful"
"I am worthy"
"I am capable"
"I am strong…"

"Be patient"
"Be still."

She had worn a hole in the floor from pacing back and forth amid the 4 am winter darkness that filled the hallways of her home.
Anyone witnessing this physical display of mental uneasiness would write her off as crazy.

And she was;
but not just any kind of crazy.

She was the kind of crazy you become after losing so much…

maybe a parent.

maybe a child.

maybe a love…

Some or all of that,
but she was definitely crazy.

So she went to pray to herself;
to bring her spirit back to her mind—
her mind back to her body—
her body back to herself—
herself back to her soul—
her soul back to God.

So she kneeled;
bowed down to write and pray to herself:

"I Am."

JOHN 10: Stay Woke

"The thief comes only to steal and kill and destroy; I have come that they may have life, and have it to the full."

For Trayvon

When I die,
do not cry for me.
Do not moan
and mourn
and waste your tears.

Do not
contemplate
my immortal soul.
Do not project your fears.

Find,
instead,
courage;
that I've
not died
in vain.

Reject
your shared
misery.
Disdain
your common
pain.

Find,
instead,

justice
Find,
instead,
peace.

Light,
for me,
no candles when I die.
But instead,

light a *fire*

for me…

Surname

I got some man's name
stamped on me.

Some man's Name—
Stamped—
on *me*…

Like a brand
stamped on a *clothing line*.
Like a *brand*
stamped on a *shoe*…
Like…
a *BRAND*…

Stamped on a *You*…

A brand;
Hot iron to cattle.

A brand;
Burning flesh to metal.

A brand…
stamped on me…
like hot iron…
on cattle…

NIGGA

What's in that word?
>"Nigga"

What's in any word…
>(Nigga)

but the power you give it?

Personification Too

Truth breaches Silence.
Truth orders Increase.
      Truth guides Light to Darkness,
      and demands: Desist and Cease.

Truth provokes Violence,
Truth completes Peace.
It judges Lies harshly,
and sentences Decrease.

Truth is no Tyrant.
Truth does not police.
Truth does not jail, You.
But *Truth*, sets You, free.

Question

[I]f I take your race away and there you are all strung out and all you got is your little self and what is that? What *are* you without racism? Are you any good? Are you still strong? Still smart? You still like yourself?" –Toni Morrison

You know what your violence is?

An eruption of your insecurities—

(the ones *you've* claimed).

Knowing that,

I feel sorry for you.

…Because no amount of

Burning

Killing

Shooting

or

Looting

Will ever make you as superior

as you wish to be…

And that comforts me.

John 10

"I tell you the truth,
the one who will sneak
and not go through
the gate (me),
he is a robber
and a thief.

He is crooked
and not straight.

But,
the one who enters
through the gate,
is the true shepherd;
the true sheep should wait.

The gatekeeper opens the gate
for him.
His sheep recognize his voice.
They come to him when called by name;
when lead,
they follow by choice.

They won't follow a stranger–
instead–
they *will*
run from him.
Unsure of his motives;
they discern
they're grim.

I tell you the truth,
I am the gate.
All before me
were thieves.

True sheep
did not listen to them,
they waited,
instead,
for me.

Yes!
I am the gate!

Those who come through me
dwell in green pastures,
where they roam for free.

I am the good shepherd;
and when you follow me,
you are fully covered
because you are my sheep.

Because you are my sheep
you are worth my life:
people for my possession;
worthy
sacrifice.

A hired hand abandons sheep
they don't belong to him.
He is not their shepherd
So:
They need
and find him gone
from them.

Then the wolves attack the flock
and scatter them astray.
Working only for the money,
selfishly
he runs away.

I am the good shepherd.
I know my sheep.
My sheep and my Father
Both know me.

I lay my life
at His feet
Of my *own*
authority.
No one takes
my life from me,
This command,
I receive.
And it's for
this very thing
That my Father

prefers me.

First John, Second Chapter; Verses 15-17

This world is not my home I'm just a-passin' through/My treasures are laid up somewhere
beyond the blue/The angels beckon me from heaven's open door/And I can't feel at home
in this world anymore.
    –"This World Is Not My Home"

We've made idols of worldly things;
of worldly aspirations,
of worldly dreams.

Above Eternal Treasures
we've placed worldly things
and we've…
become lovers of the world
it seems.

We've ex-changed diamond mines
for borrowed bling.

Traded Kings on Thrones
for puppets on strings;

surrendered Crystal Waters
for polluted plastic springs

renounced Milk and Honey
for depleted brooks and streams.

We reject honesty and honor,
and opt for plots and schemes.

We scoff at faithfulness and fidelity,
and philander in acts unclean.

We forsake our children's minds;
consign them to screens
neglect their spirit
because
we haven't our own to bring.

We deny the Supreme,
Crucify the redeemed;
sacrifice our souls,

our sense of self-worth,
and our self- esteem.

We're Covetous.
We're Foolish.
We're Filthy
and we're weak—
doing things
in the dark
too shameful
to even speak.

Fall
on your knees!
Remember
who to please.

That
of the world,
is not
of Me.

"No man can love God,
AND
the world,"
said He;

"If anyone love the world,
he can't also love the Three."

Idle Worship

Do not let anyone who delights in false humility and the worship of angels disqualify you. Such a person also goes into great detail about what they have seen; they are puffed up with idle notions by their unspiritual mind. They have lost connection with the head, from whom the whole body, supported and held together by its ligaments and sinews, grows as God causes it to grow.

—Colossians 2:18-19

XVIII

Emotions make them uncomfortable,
so they go through life not feeling.

Pain makes them tired,
so they go through life not dealing.

Numb, they're left lifeless,
so they go through life
not healing.

No joy to call their own,
so they go through life
just stealing.

Mothers can't love daughters.
Fathers can't love sons.
Elders lying to us,
hiding what they've done.

Lovers hate each other,
Siblings fuss and fight.

No love extended,
no care in sight.

What we call evil,
They call it good.
They partake with whom they shouldn't,
and shun whom they should.

Constantly making each other sad;
making each other bitter and mad.
Willing down generational pain,
soiling hearts crimson with stains.

XIX

Heads and eyes lowered;
bowed as he's praying.
Ears tuned in
to the words that he's saying.
Hands in the air,
No idea,
no clue.

Mind sealed shut
to the messages coming through.

Father, Son, Holy Ghost—
tell us what to do.

"Jesus,
Jehovah Jireh
speak—
we're
waiting
on *You.*"

Daybreak In Mississippi

Good morning, Sun,
How I've missed your light.

How I've longed for you in
dark hours of the night.

How all seemed wrong,
and nothing seemed right.
How dreadful and dreary
seemed my plight.

How defeated I'd felt;
surrendered the fight
Filled with fear,
uncertainty and fright.

Gone you seemed,
out of my sight
Until you shone,
victorious and bright.

Rose to your throne,
to heavens' height.
Covered in warmth;
filled with might.

Transcended
perpetual
darkness
and blight
Bid me bid defeat
"goodnight"!

From my sleep
you woke me,
to praise you and write:

"Good morning, Sun.
OH!
How I missed your light."

Amen.

www.ingramcontent.com/pod-product-compliance
Lightning Source LLC
Chambersburg PA
CBHW031423250726
48656CB00002B/805